A LIF

JULIAN BARNES

A LIFE WITH BOOKS

JONATHAN CAPE

LONDON

Published by Jonathan Cape 2012

2 4 6 8 10 9 7 5 3 1

Copyright © Julian Barnes

First published in Great Britain in 2012 by Jonathan Cape
Random House, 20 Vauxhall Bridge Road,
London SW1V 2SA

www.randomhouse.co.uk

Addresses for companies within The Random House Group Limited
can be found at: www.randomhouse.co.uk/offices.htm

The Random House Group Limited Reg. No. 954009

A CIP catalogue record for this book is available
from the British Library

ISBN 9780224097260

The Random House Group Limited makes every effort to
ensure that the papers used in its books are made from trees that have
been legally sourced from well-managed and credibly certified forests.
Our paper procurement policy can be found at:
www.randomhouse.co.uk/paper.htm

Printed and bound in Great Britain by
the MPG Books Group

I HAVE LIVED IN BOOKS, for books, by and with books; in recent years, I have been fortunate enough to be able to live from books. And it was through books that I first realized there were other worlds beyond my own; first imagined what it might be like to be another person; first encountered that deeply intimate bond made when a writer's voice gets inside a reader's head. I was perhaps lucky that for the first ten years of my life there was no competition from television; and when one finally arrived into the household, it was under the strict control of my parents. They were both schoolteachers, so respect for the book and what it contained were implicit.

We didn't go to church, but we did go to the library.

My maternal grandparents were also teachers. Grandpa had a mail-order set of Dickens and a *Nelson's Encyclopaedia* in about twenty-five small red volumes. My parents had classier and more varied books, and in later life became members of the Folio Society. I grew up assuming that all homes contained books; that this was normal. It was normal, too, that they were valued for their usefulness: to learn from at school, to dispense and verify information, and to entertain during the holidays. My father had collections of *Times* Fourth Leaders; my mother might enjoy a Nancy Mitford. Their shelves also contained the leather-bound prizes my father had won at Ilkeston County School between

1921 and 1925, mostly for 'General Proficiency' or 'General Excellence': *The Pageant of English Prose*, Goldsmith's *Poetical Works*, Cary's Dante, Lytton's *Last of the Barons*, Charles Reade's *The Cloister and the Hearth*.

None of these works excited me as a boy. I first started investigating my parents' shelves (and those of my grandparents, and of my older brother) when awareness of sex dawned. Grandpa's library contained little lubricity except a scene or two in John Masters's *Bhowani Junction*; my parents had William Orpen's *The Outline of Art* with several important black-and-white illustrations; but my brother owned a copy of Petronius's *Satyricon*, which was the hottest book by far on the home shelves. The Romans definitely led a more riotous life than the one I witnessed around me in Northwood, Middlesex. Banquets, slave girls, orgies, all sorts of stuff. I wonder if my brother noticed that after a while some of the pages of his *Satyricon* were almost falling from the spine. Foolishly, I assumed that all his ancient classics must have similar erotic content. I spent many a dull day with his Hesiod before concluding that this wasn't the case.

The local high street included an establishment we referred to as 'the bookshop'. In fact, it was a fancy-goods store plus stationer's with a downstairs room, about half of which was given over to books. Some of them were quite respectable – Penguin classics, Penguin and Pan fiction. Part of me assumed that these were all the books that there were. I mean, I knew there were different books in the public library, and there were school books, which were again different; but in terms of the wider world of books, I assumed this tiny sample was somehow representative. Occasionally, in another suburb or town, we might visit a 'real' bookshop, which usually turned out to be a branch of W.H. Smith.

The only variant book-source came if you won a school prize (I was at City of London School, then on Victoria Embankment next to Blackfriars Bridge). Winners were allowed to choose their own books, usually under parental supervision. But again, this was somehow a narrowing rather than a broadening exercise. You could choose them only from a selection available at a private showroom in an office block on the South Bank: a place both slightly mysterious and utterly functional. It was, I later discovered, yet another part of W.H.Smith. Here were books of weight and worthiness, the sort to be admired rather than perhaps ever read. Your school prize would have a particular value, you chose a book for up to that amount, whereupon it vanished from your sight, to reappear on Lord Mayor's Prize Day, when the Lord Mayor of London, in full regalia, would personally hand it over to you. Now it would contain a pasted-in page on the front endpaper describing your achievement, while the cloth cover bore the gilt-embossed school arms. I can remember little of what I obediently chose when guided by my parents. But in 1963 I won the Mortimer English prize, and, being now seventeen, must have gone by myself to that depository of seriousness, where I found (whose slip-up could it have been?) a copy of *Ulysses*. I can still see the disapproving face of the Lord Mayor as his protectively gloved hand passed over to me this notoriously filthy novel.

By now, I was beginning to view books as more than just utilitarian: sources of information, instruction, delight or titillation. First there was the excitement and meaning of possession. To own a certain book — and to choose it without help — was to define yourself. And that self-definition had to be protected, physically. So I would cover my favourite books (paperbacks, inevitably, out of financial constraint) with transparent Fablon. First, though, I would write my name — in a recently-acquired italic hand, in blue ink, underlined with red — on the edge of the inside cover. The Fablon would then be cut and fitted so that it also covered and protected the ownership signature. Some of these books – for instance, David Magarshak's Penguin translations of the Russian classics – are still on my shelves.

Self-definition was one kind of magic. And then I was slowly introduced to another kind: that of the old, the secondhand, the non-new book. I remember a line of Auden first editions in the glass-fronted bookcase of a neighbour: a man, moreover, who had actually known Auden decades previously, and even played cricket with him. These facts seemed to me astonishing. I had never set eyes on a writer, or known anyone who had known a writer. I might have heard one or two on the wireless, seen one or two on television in a 'Face to Face' interview with John

Freeman. But our family's nearest connection to Literature was the fact that my father had read modern languages at Nottingham University, where the Professor was Ernest Weekley, whose wife had run off with D.H. Lawrence. Oh, and my mother had once seen R.D. Smith, husband of Olivia Manning, on a Birmingham station platform. Yet here were the ownership copies of someone who had known one of the country's most famous living poets. Further, these books contained Auden's still-echoing words in the form in which they had first come into the world. I sensed this magic sharply, and wanted part of it. So, from my student years, I became a book-collector as well as a book-user, and discovered that bookshops weren't all owned by W.H.Smith.

Over the next decade or so – from the late Sixties to the late Seventies – I became a furious book-hunter, driving to the market towns and cathedral cities of England in my Morris Traveller and loading it with books bought at a rate which far exceeded any possible reading speed. This was a time when most towns of reasonable size had at least one large, long-established secondhand bookshop, often found within the shadow of the cathedral or city church; as I remember, you could usually park right outside for as long as you wanted. Without exception these would be independently owned shops – sometimes with a selection of new books at the front – and I immediately felt at home in them. The atmosphere, for a start, was so different. Here books seemed to be valued, and to form part of a continuing culture. By now, I probably preferred secondhand books to new ones. In America such items were disparagingly referred to as 'previously owned'; but this very continuity of ownership was part of their charm. A book dispensed its explanation of the world to one person, then another, and so on down the generations; different hands held the same book and drew sometimes the same, sometimes a different wisdom from it. Old books showed their age: they had fox-marks the way old people had liver-spots. They also smelt good – even when they reeked of cigarettes and (occasionally) cigars. And many might disgorge pungent ephemera: ancient publishers' announcements and old bookmarks – often for insurance companies or Sunlight soap.

So I would drive to Salisbury, Petersfield, Aylesbury, Southport, Cheltenham, Guildford, getting into back rooms and locked warehouses and storesheds whenever I could. I was much less at ease in places which smelt of fine bindings, or which knew all too well the value of each item for sale. I preferred the democratic clutter of a shop whose stock was roughly ordered and where bargains were possible. In those days, even in shops selling new books, there was none of the ferociously fast turnaround that modern central management imposes. Nowadays, the average shelf life of a new hardback novel – assuming it can reach a shelf in the first place – is four months. Then, books would stay on the shelves until someone bought them, or they might be reluctantly put into a special sale, or moved to the secondhand department, where they might rest for years on end. That book you couldn't afford, or weren't sure you really wanted, would often still be there on your return trip the following year. Secondhand shops demonstrated how severe posterity's judgement often turns out to be. Charles Morgan, Hugh Walpole, Dornford Yates, Lord Lytton, Mrs Henry Wood – there would be yards and yards of them out there, waiting for fashion to turn again. It rarely did.

I bought with a hunger which I recognise, looking back, was a kind of neediness: well, bibliomania is a known condition. Book-buying certainly consumed more than half of my disposable income. I bought first editions of the writers I most admired: Waugh, Greene,

Huxley, Durrell, Betjeman. I bought first editions of Victorian poets like Tennyson and Browning (neither of whom I had read) because they seemed astonishingly cheap. The dividing line between books I liked, books I thought I would like, books I hoped I would like, and books I didn't like now but thought I might at some future date was rarely distinct. I collected King Penguins, Batsford books on the countryside, and the *Britain in Pictures* series produced by Collins in the 1940s and 1950s. I bought poetry pamphlets and leather-backed French encyclopaedias published by Larousse; cartoon books and Victorian keepsakes; out-of-date dictionaries and bound copies of magazines from the *Cornhill* to the *Strand*. I bought a copy of *Sensation!*, the first Belgian edition of Waugh's

Scoop. I even made up a category called Odd Books, used to justify eccentric purchases such as Sir Robert Baden-Powell's *Pig-Sticking or Hog-Hunting*, Bombadier Billy Wells's *Physical Energy*, Cheiro's *Guide to the Hand*, and *Tap-Dancing Made Easy* by 'Isolde'. All are still on my shelves, if rarely consulted. I also bought books it made no sense to buy, either at the time or in retrospect – like all three volumes (in first edition, with dust-wrappers, and definitely unread by the previous owner) of Sir Anthony Eden's memoirs. Where was the sense in that? My case was made worse by the fact that I was, in the jargon of the trade, a completist. So, for instance, because I had admired the few plays of Shaw that I'd seen, I ended up with several feet of his work, even down to obscure pamphlets about vegetarianism.

Since Shaw was so popular, and his print-runs accordingly vast, I never paid much for any of this collection. Which also meant that when, thirty years later, having become less keen on Shaw's didacticism and self-conscious wit, I decided to sell out, a clear minus profit was made.

Occasionally, there were thrilling discoveries. In the back warehouse of F. Weatherhead & Son of Aylesbury I found a copy of the first two cantos of Byron's *Don Juan*, published without the author's name in 1819. This rare first edition, bound in blue cloth, cost me 12/6d (or 62.5p). I would like to pretend (as I occasionally used to) that it was my specialist knowledge of Byronic bibliography that led me to spot it. But this would have been to ignore the full pencil note from the bookseller inside the front cover (*'Cantos I and II appeared in London in July 1819 without the name of either author or bookseller in a thin quarto'*). The price of 12/6d therefore couldn't have been an oversight; more likely, it was an indication that the book had been on the shelves for decades.

Just as often, however, I would make serious mistakes. Why, for instance, did I buy, from D.M. Beach of Salisbury, *Oliver Twist* in its original monthly parts, as first issued by *Bentley's Miscellany*? It was a good idea because they were in perfect condition, with fine plates, covers and advertisements. It was a bad idea because one of the parts (either the first or last) was missing – hence the set's near-affordability. It was an optimistic idea because I was sure I would be able to track down the missing part at some moment in my collecting life. Needless to say, I never did, and this idiocy rebuked me from my shelves for many years.

Then there were moments when I realized that the world of books and book-collecting was not exactly as I'd imagined it. While I was familiar with famous cases of book forgery, I always assumed that collectors were honest and straightforward folk (I used to think the same about gardeners too). Then, one day, I found myself at the Lilies in Weedon, Bucks — 'by appointment only' — a thirty-five-room Victorian mansion so stuffed with books that a visit occupied most of the day. Among its first-edition section I found a book I had been chasing for years: Evelyn Waugh's *Vile Bodies*. It lacked a dustwrapper (which was normal — few early Waugh-buyers failed to discard the jackets), but was in pristine condition. The price was . . . astonishingly low. Then I read a little pencilled note which explained why. It was in the handwriting, and with the signature, of Roger Senhouse, the Bloomsburyite publisher who was Lytton Strachey's last lover. It read – and I quote from memory – 'This second impression was left on my shelves in the place of my own first edition.' I was deeply shocked. Clearly, it had not been a spur-of-the-moment act. The culprit must have arrived *chez* Senhouse with this copy concealed about him – I assumed it was a he not a she – and then managed the switch when no one was in the room. Who could it have been? Might I ever be tempted to such action? (Yes, I subsequently was – tempted, that is.) And might someone do that to me and my collection one day? (Not as far as I know.)

More recently, I heard another version of this story, from a different point of view. A reader sent a rather famous living author a copy of an early novel of his (one whose first print-run was under a thousand copies), asking for a signature and enclosing return postage. After a while, a parcel arrived containing the novel, duly signed by the author – except that he had retained the valuable first edition and sent a second impression instead.

Back then, book-hunting involved high mileage, slow accumulation and frequent frustration; the side-effect was a tendency, when failing to find what you wanted, to buy a scattershot array of stuff to prove that your journey hadn't been wasted. This manner of acquisition is no longer possible, or no longer makes sense. All those old, rambling, beautifully-sited shops have gone. Here is Roy Harley Lewis's *The Book-Browser's Guide to Secondhand and Antiquarian Bookshops* (second edition, 1982) on D.M. Beach of Salisbury: 'There are a number of bookshops on sites so valuable that the proprietors could realise a small fortune by selling up and working from home . . . While property prices in Wiltshire cannot compare with (say) London, this marvellous corner site in the High Street is an enormous overhead for any bookshop.' Beach's closed in 1999; Weatherhead's (which had its own printed paper bag) in 1998; the Lilies – which was full of stray exhibits such as John Cowper Powys's death-mask and 'the clock that belonged to the people who put the engine in the boat that Shelley drowned in' – is no more. The bigger, and the more general, the more vulnerable, seems to have been the rule.

Collecting has also been changed utterly by the Internet. It took me perhaps a dozen years to find a first edition of *Vile Bodies* for about £25. Today, thirty seconds with abebooks.com will turn up two dozen first editions of varied condition and price (the most expensive, with that rarest of Waugh dustwrappers, run from $15,000 to $28,000). When the great English novelist Penelope Fitzgerald died, I decided as homage to buy first editions (with dustwrappers) of her last four novels – the four that established her greatness. This all took less time than it would to find a parking space nowadays near the spot where Beach's bookshop used to exist. And while I could go on about the Romance and Serendipity of Discovery – and yes, there was romance – the old system was neither time- nor cost-effective.

I became a bit less of a book-collector (or, perhaps, book-fetishist) after I published my first novel. Perhaps, at some subconscious level, I decided that since I was now producing my own first editions, I needed other people's less. I even started to sell books, which once would have seemed inconceivable. Not that this has slowed my rate of acquisition: I still buy books faster than I can read them. But again, this feels completely normal: how weird it would be to have around you only as many books as you have time to read in the rest of your life.

And I remain deeply attached to the physical book and the physical bookshop. The current pressures on both are enormous. My last novel would have cost you £12.99 in a bookshop, about half that (plus postage) online, and a mere £4.79 as a Kindle download. The economics seem unanswerable. Yet, fortunately, economics have never entirely controlled either reading or book-buying. John Updike, towards the end of his life, became pessimistic about the future of the printed book:

> For who, in that unthinkable future
> When I am dead, will read? The printed page
> Was just a half-millennium's brief wonder . . .

I am more optimistic, both about reading and about books. There will always be nonreaders, bad readers, lazy readers — there always were. Reading is a majority skill but a minority art. Yet nothing can replace the exact, complicated, subtle communion between absent author and entranced, present reader. Nor do I think the e-reader will ever completely supplant the physical book — even if it does so numerically. Every book feels and looks different in your hands; every Kindle download feels and looks exactly the same (though perhaps the e-reader will one day contain a 'smell' function, which you will click to make your electronic Dickens novel suddenly reek of damp paper, fox-marks and nicotine). Books will have to earn their keep — and so will bookshops. Books will have to become more desirable: not luxury goods, but well-designed, attractive, making us want to pick them up, buy them, give them as presents, keep them, think about rereading them, and remember in later years that this was the edition in which we first encountered what lay inside. I have no Luddite prejudice against new technology; it's just that books look as if they contain knowledge, while e-readers look as if they contain information. My father's school prizes are nowadays on my shelves, ninety years after he first won them. I'd rather read Goldsmith's poems in this form than online.

The American writer and dilettante Logan Pearsall Smith once said: 'Some people think that life is the thing; but I prefer reading.' When I first came across this, I thought it witty; now I find it – as I do many aphorisms – a slick untruth. Life and reading are not separate activities. The distinction is false (as it is when Yeats imagines the writer's choice between 'perfection of the life, or of the work'). When you read a great book, you don't escape from life, you plunge deeper into it. There may be a superficial escape – into different countries, mores, speech patterns – but what you are essentially doing is furthering your understanding of life's subtleties, paradoxes, joys, pains and truths. Reading and life are not separate but symbiotic. And for this serious task of imaginative discovery and self-discovery, there is and remains one perfect symbol: the printed book.